Out There — Travel

ELIZABETH BARDSWICH • MIRIAM BARDSWICH

Editorial Board
David Booth • Joan Green • Jack Booth

Steck-Vaughn
A Harcourt Achieve Imprint

10801 N. Mopac Expressway
Building # 3
Austin, TX 78759
1.800.531.5015

Steck-Vaughn is a trademark of Harcourt Achieve Inc. registered in the
United States of America and/or other jurisdictions. All inquiries should be
mailed to Harcourt Achieve Inc., P.O. Box 27010, Austin, TX 78755.

Rubicon © 2007 Rubicon Publishing Inc.
www.rubiconpublishing.com

Associate Publisher: Miriam Bardswich
Editor: Dona Foucault
Creative/Art Director: Jennifer Drew
Senior Designer: Jeanette MacLean

Cover Image–Getty Images/Stone/Frank Herholdt; Title Page Image–Shutterstock

7 8 9 10 11 5 4 3 2 1

Out There — Travel
ISBN: 978-1-4190-4030-6

CONTENTS

Adventure awaits —
For those who seek to travel
The world is

Out there

Wish You Were

warm up

If you were traveling, what kind of hotel would you like to stay in?

Ottawa

POSTCARD

Ottawa, Ontario
C A N A D A

Hey, Billy! What's up?
Spent the night in jail .... a former jail, that is. The Carleton County Gaol, which is now a hostel right in downtown Ottawa. You sleep in a real jail cell. The building is supposedly haunted by Patrick James Whelan, who was publicly hanged here. Talk about history! Yesterday I saw the Parliament Buildings. Next I'm on to Montreal to check out the old city.

See you soon buddy.
Sanjaya

Bill

181 E

Chica

ICE HOTEL

JUKKASJARVI
Swedish Lapland

Hello, Sis! Greetings from the frozen North. Think you're pretty cool? Try staying in an ice hotel. This is the original one and the world's largest. Everything is made of crystal-clear ice, including the artwork. The beds and chairs are covered with reindeer hides. And a good thing, too! Next, I'm going to check out the ice hotel in La Belle Province, near Québec City,

See you soon!
Miss ya.
Femi

789

Toro

Here!

Osaka, Japan
Osaka Castle - Osaka at night - Japanese girls in kimonos

Hi, Alina,

Greetings from Japan! What a wonderful country. Last night I slept in a capsule. Nothing to do with outer space — this was a capsule hotel. There are no rooms, just units grouped together and stacked one on top of another. Just enough room to sleep. Good thing I don't suffer from claustrophobia!

Love,
Uncle Antosha

OSAKA, JAPAN

Miss Alina Fabri

46 C

Sandi

CHECKPOINT
How would you define this?

Foulksrath Castle
Kilkenny, Ireland

Hi, Nick,

Guess what? We stayed in a haunted castle last night. It was built in the 16th century, but is now a youth hostel. Huge fireplaces, spiral staircases, and a chance to see a ghost. We didn't see one, but one of our roommates says she did (yeah, right). We met people from all over the world — too bad you couldn't come. We'll tell you all about it when we get home.

Meg and Amanda

Nick

9 A

Su

Foulksrath Castle

7

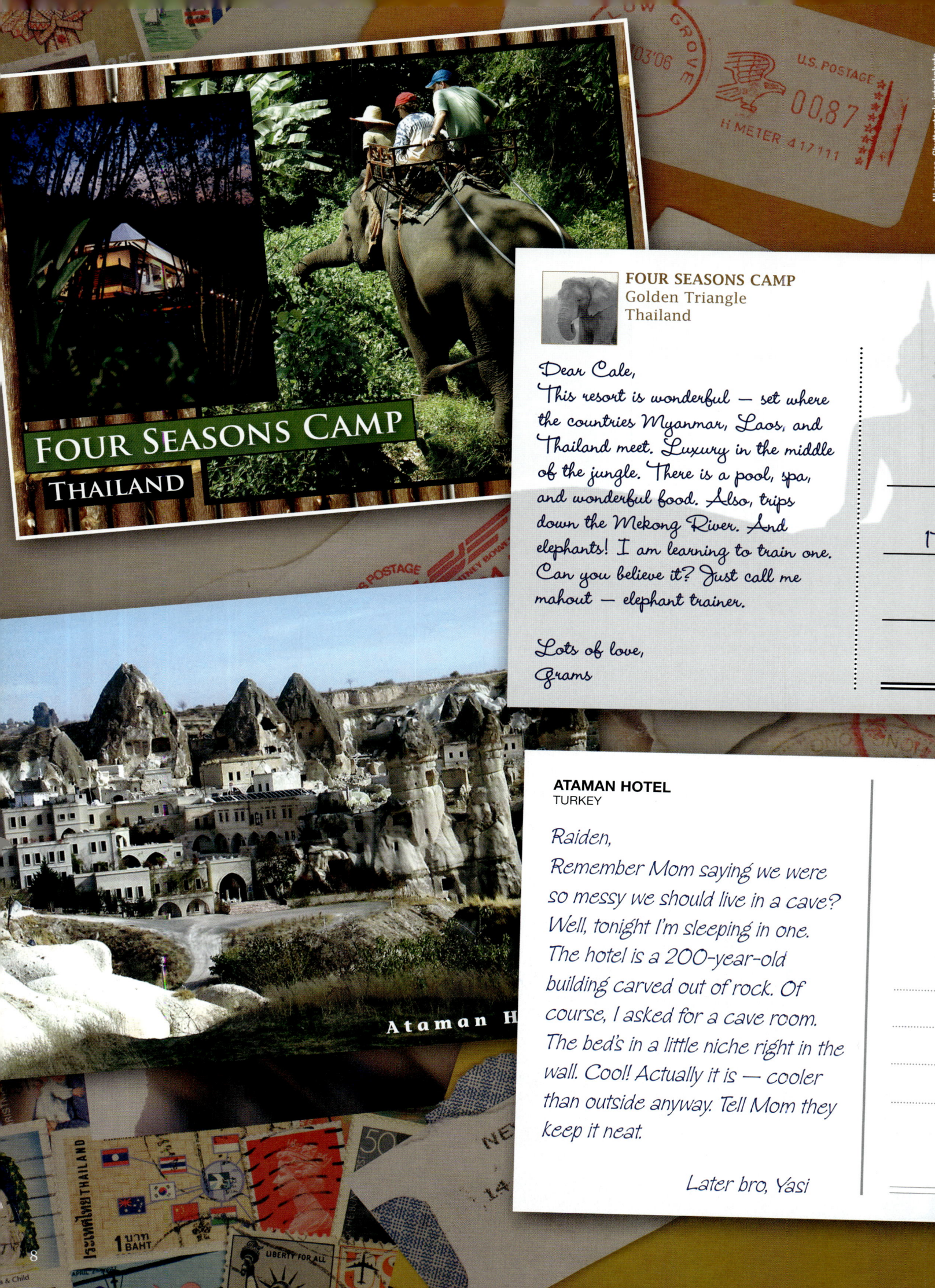

FOUR SEASONS CAMP
Golden Triangle
Thailand

Dear Cale,
This resort is wonderful — set where the countries Myanmar, Laos, and Thailand meet. Luxury in the middle of the jungle. There is a pool, spa, and wonderful food. Also, trips down the Mekong River. And elephants! I am learning to train one. Can you believe it? Just call me mahout — elephant trainer.

Lots of love,
Grams

ATAMAN HOTEL
TURKEY

Raiden,
Remember Mom saying we were so messy we should live in a cave? Well, tonight I'm sleeping in one. The hotel is a 200-year-old building carved out of rock. Of course, I asked for a cave room. The bed's in a little niche right in the wall. Cool! Actually it is — cooler than outside anyway. Tell Mom they keep it neat.

Later bro, Yasi

Hotels in lighthouses, castles, caves, treetops, ships — staying at any of these would be an adventure. But for a really unique experience, try spending the night underground or underwater.

The Desert Cave Hotel at Coober Pedy, Australia, offers 50 underground suites — spacious, dark, and cool, great for sleeping. Of course, half of the people who live in Coober Pedy live, shop, and go to school underground.

spacious: roomy

At Jules Undersea Lodge in Florida, hotel guests arrive by scuba diving 21 feet below the ocean surface. At the new Hydropolis in Dubai, United Arab Emirates, guests can connect to the 200-suite submarine hotel via a tunnel from a land station.

COOBER PEDY

Hydropolis

wrap up

1. Which of the hotels featured in the postcards interests you the most? Rank the hotels from 1 to 6 with #1 being your favorite. Explain why in one sentence for each.

2. Choose three of the hotels and write a question that you would like to ask the person who stayed there.

WEB CONNECTIONS

Go online to research one of the hotels identified in the sidebar or another unusual hotel. Imagine that you have stayed at the hotel and write a postcard to a person of your choice.

MULE RIDE WITH A VIEW

By Catherine Pike

Mule ride photos–courtesy Conner Wiebe

warm up

Look at the images on these pages. Do you think you would try this adventure?

Connor's view from the saddle of his mule

Tourists can also hike into the Grand Canyon or ride horses into some parts of it. There are float tours and river rafting on the Colorado River and helicopter and airplane tours over the canyon. For the less adventurous, companies offer bus, jeep, and steam train rides along the rim of the canyon.

Climbing the canyon wall

8:00 AM at the Stone Corral

My mule was named Skidmark, a name I didn't have time to ponder as we mounted up and started our steep descent into the Grand Canyon. With the mules taking the outermost edge of the trail and the first of many hair-raising switchbacks behind us, I was definitely having second thoughts about … an eight-hour trail ride into the depths of the canyon. My youngest son, Connor, 11, turned around in his saddle and said, "This is the best thing I've ever done in my life!" It was definitely an adventure and not for the faint of heart.

ponder: *think carefully*
switchbacks: *sharp bends on a zigzag road or trail*
faint of heart: *lacking courage*

Descent view of the Grand Canyon

11

Grand Canyon Mule Ride

LENGTH OF RIDES
- Half-day to three-day rides into the canyon
- One-hour rides along the rim of the canyon

RIDER RESTRICTIONS
- Height: 4'7" or taller
- Weight: 200 lbs. or less, fully dressed
- Must be fit

TRAILS
- Narrow, above steep cliffs
- Many switchbacks

SAFETY
- Mules walk close to the edge of the cliffs but they are sure-footed and accidents are rare.

While we were still within the safe confines of the corral, my husband, Eric, chose to declare a problem with heights as he mounted a huge mule named Goldie. He spent much of the trip down and back up the steep canyon walls staring at the ground in fear! There are some restrictions for mule riding. Riders must be under a certain weight and we all had to step onto a big scale before we were certified fit to ride.

CHECKPOINT

Check out the sidebar for rider restrictions.

Halfway down the canyon, we stopped at Indian Garden to water the mules and stretch our legs. As I dismounted, I was shocked to find I could barely walk. My legs had been gripping the mule tightly for three hours and had become rubbery, refusing to do my bidding — a simple request — to walk into the shade and have a drink of water from the canteen I was given at the outset of our ride. The trail boss pointed out it was usually 115º F at Plateau Point in the summer. A dry heat of course. Being March break, we found it cool and sunny and enjoyed the breeze from the canyon floor while eating our box lunches looking down on the Colorado River from the canyon edge. Our family had completed the Bright Angel Trail — quite an accomplishment.

canteen: *small container for carrying liquids*

View of Bright Angel Trail

Lunch beside a sheer drop to the canyon floor

Later, we drove to Flagstaff, Arizona, visited the Meteor Crater, stopping briefly at the Four Corners, where my sons took turns having pictures taken while in four states at the same time. One foot in New Mexico, the other in Arizona, a hand in Utah, and one in Colorado! We then headed for the Navajo Nation and its surreal Monument Valley. The ordinary world slides away as you approach the valley. You leave the van and worship at sandstone temples to the sky. It's not really weather that did this, nor even energy, but time. The Ear of the Wind was a truly amazing geological formation.

Snow greeted us at Ruby's Inn high in Bryce Canyon, Utah, before our descent through Zion National Park to the Hoover Dam and finally Las Vegas.

surreal: *unreal, fantastic*

Connor pictured at Monument Valley

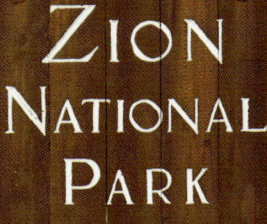
Bryce Canyon

wrap up

1. List the words and phrases used by the author to describe the mule ride into the Grand Canyon. Study the images. What words and phrases would you use? Add these to the list.

2. Write an e-mail that the author or one of her sons might have sent to a friend back home that would make him or her want to travel to the Grand Canyon.

WEB CONNECTIONS

Use the Web to research and create a collage of images from other places that the family visited on their March break vacation. Give the collage a catchy title.

ZION NATIONAL PARK
U.S. DEPARTMENT OF THE INTERIOR
NATIONAL PARK SERVICE

NATIONAL PARK SERVICE
Department of the Interior

Travel

By Robert Louis Stevenson

warm up

Have you read any books by Robert Louis Stevenson, such as *Treasure Island* or *Kidnapped*? Some of his stories have been made into movies. Share what you know with a partner.

CHECKPOINT

Are you familiar with Daniel Dafoe's story *Robinson Crusoe* or the movie *Castaway*?

I should like to rise and go
Where the golden apples grow;
Where below another sky
Parrot islands anchored lie,
And, watched by cockatoos and goats,
Lonely Crusoes building boats; —
Where in sunshine reaching out
Eastern cities, miles about,
Are with mosque and minaret
Among sandy gardens set,
And the rich goods from near and far
Hang for sale in the bazaar; —

minaret: *slender tower of a mosque*
bazaar: *marketplace*

Where the Great Wall round China goes,
And on one side the desert blows,
And with the voice and bell and drum,
Cities on the other hum; —
Where are forests hot as fire,
Wide as England, tall as a spire, ...
Where the knotty crocodile
Lies and blinks in the Nile,
And the red flamingo flies
Hunting fish before his eyes;
Where in jungles near and far,
Man-devouring tigers are,
Lying close and giving ear
Lest the hunt be drawing near,
Or a comer-by be seen
Swinging in the palanquin; –
Where among the desert sands
Some deserted city stands, ...

spire: *tapering roof or tower*
palanquin: *curtained couch mounted on pieces
of wood, used to carry one passenger on the
shoulders of at least two other people*

CHECKPOINT
What do you think this means?

wrap up

1. Choose one scene from the poem and visualize
   the setting. Sketch the scene or imagine you are
   there and describe the scene for your group.

2. Imagine that, in your travels, you discover a
   deserted island or a deserted city in the desert.
   Write an announcement that a TV host might
   give for a show about your discovery.

WEB CONNECTIONS

Use the Web to find a biography of
Robert Louis Stevenson. Check out the
many books, poems, and songs that he
wrote. Which work appeals to you the
most? What is it about? Present your
findings and explain your choice to
your group or class.

COSTA RICA

warm up

Look at the images on these pages. Jot down words to describe Costa Rica.

There is a land where you can stand on top of a mountain and look at both the Atlantic and Pacific oceans. It's a land where you can soar through the mists above a cloud forest or listen to howler monkeys as you raft down jungle rivers.

Costa Rica — "rich coast" — named by Christopher Columbus in 1502, is a small, peaceful Central American country. This is one of the world's major vacation spots with about one million visitors every year. Here you can travel from the ocean to the jungle to the mountains in the same day. Volcanoes, rain forests, and pristine beaches are the norm.

Costa Rica caters especially to the environmentally-wise visitor who is looking for adventure. The word ecotourism was coined here in what is one of the most biodiverse areas in the world. Costa Rica offers many eco-friendly tours and sights.

CHECKPOINT
What do you think these might be?

Take a trip to one of the most popular destinations, the Monteverde Cloud Forest Reserve, located north of San José, the capital city of Costa Rica. Cloud forests are formed as warm, wet air from over the ocean is forced upward by mountains and then cools. The plant life in a cloud forest is unbelievable — giant trees

pristine: *unspoiled; clean as if new*
ecotourism: *travel having little impact on the environment*
biodiverse: *having a wide variety of plants and animals*

All images–Shutterstock, istockphoto

Bird-of-paradise

Sloth

Cloud forest

Hummingbird

Orchid

Baby margay

Parrot

Manuel Antonio

Pineapple field

Butterfly

Spider monkey

17

Zip line

Suspension walkway

form a huge canopy with vines, orchids, ferns, and all manner of plants. Some of the tropical plants that you see in your local supermarket or florist shop grow as tall as 90 feet here. Wildlife is abundant in this majestic jungle and you can spend all day hiking the trails, hoping to spot an ocelot, jaguar, some of the 500 species of butterfly, or that rare bird — the quetzal.

A highlight of a Costa Rican vacation is a ride on the zip line. Very knowledgeable Costa Rican guides take tourists on trails leading up the mountain to platforms erected high in the rain forest canopy. A steel cable stretches from platform to platform. A guide helps you into a harness and a pulley connects you to the cable. You zip along the cable, literally disappearing into the cloud forest mist.

CHECKPOINT
Would you try the zip line?

canopy: *covering*

This ride is not for the faint of heart! If you decide the zip line is not for you, you can walk back down the mountain using the trails and suspension walkways. These walkways give you an excellent look at the forest and the chance to see rare butterflies, hummingbirds, and orchids.

North of Monteverde is Arenal Lake, a cool, human-made mountain lake. This is the spot for water sports, especially windsurfing and fishing. Just be very careful! Local folklore says that Arenal Lake has its very own monster. A large, hairy, serpent-like creature is believed to live in the watery depths!

CHECKPOINT
Picture the creature. What does it look like?

FYI

The quetzal is a bird that has brilliant bronze-green and red plumage and, in the male, long, flowing tail feathers. The quetzal is endangered due to loss of habitat.

Pacuare River

Horseback riding

Walking along the trails

And at one end of the lake is a volcano, which suddenly started erupting in 1968. Lava spews forth almost daily, but the spectacular show is at night when the eruptions turn the sky red and are reflected in the lake.

From Arenal Lake, travel eastward to the Pacuare River where you can experience some of the best in white-water rafting. This river starts in the mountains, races over rapids and through swamps, and finally rushes to the Caribbean Sea. Wearing a helmet and life preserver, you will experience a heart-pounding ride through the roaring white water. If this is not for you, relax on the white beaches in the area. Or journey north a brief

way to Tortuguero to observe hundreds of bird species and watch turtles nest.

Travel throughout this magnificent land by bus, car, four-wheeler, on horseback, or on foot. Soar above coffee plantations and pineapple fields in a hot-air balloon, or kayak around the islands of the Nicoya Peninsula. This country will give you an adventure that you will never forget. Just remember to walk carefully in Costa Rica. Ten percent of this country is national park land and almost one-quarter of the land in Costa Rica is protected from logging and the use of pesticides. Preserving the environment is very important to the people who inhabit this wonderful piece of Earth.

wrap up

1. Imagine that you are visiting Costa Rica. Write diary entries about two different activities you experienced.

2. In a small group, create a three-fold travel brochure on Costa Rica for a travel agency.

WEB CONNECTIONS

Search the Web for interesting facts about Costa Rica that you didn't read about in this article. Choose three, and write them up in the same format as the FYI.

THE BLACK HOLE OF XIBALBA

ILLUSTRATED BY FRANCESCO FRANCAVILLA '06

DAY 1: SIMON, JORGE, AND TRISH ARE CANOEING AT BARTON CREEK CAVES, IN CAYO, BELIZE.

THIS IS AWESOME, HUH?

YEAH — ARE WE STILL HITTING THE BLACK HOLE TOMORROW?

YOU KNOW IT!

DAY 2: EN ROUTE TO THE BLACK HOLE OF XIEALBA WITH THEIR TOUR GUIDE, CARLOS.

WHAT'S THE NAME OF THIS PLACE AGAIN?

AUCTUN LOCH TUNICH IS THE MAYAN NAME.

THEY BELIEVED IT LED TO *XIBALBA* — THE UNDERWORLD.

THEY TRAVEL THROUGH THICK JUNGLE.

SNAKE!

CARLOS, SERPIENTE, FER DE LANCE!

GASP!

IT'S BEAUTIFUL DOWN HERE!

A SHORT WHILE LATER ...

THIS IS AWESOME!

WE MADE IT!

CHEERS!

NOW HOW DO WE GET OUT OF HERE?

wrap up

Which of the caving activities would you most like to try? Least like to try? Why? Share your choices and reasons with a partner.

WEB CONNECTIONS

Go online to find images and descriptions of the Belize caves and the Black Hole of Xibalba. Create a poster advertising a caving adventure trip to Belize.

Wonderful

warm up

Why do you think the great waterfalls of the world are among the most visited tourist sites?

Angel Falls

AKA: *Salto Angel* in Spanish

LOCATION: Venezuela — on the River Churan in Canaima National Park

CLAIM TO FAME: Highest free-falling waterfall in the world — 3,212 feet. The water plunges straight down from the top of Anyan-Tepui or "Devil's Mountain" which is a tepuyi or table mountain.

GETTING THERE: By boat up the River Churan and a one-hour hike to the base of the falls. There is no direct road to the falls and fly-ins are expensive.

BEST VIEWS: During the rainy season — the more water, the more spectacular the falls. In the dry season, Angel Falls is almost a trickle.

ACTIVITIES: Air flights past the falls, hiking, swimming, ecotourism, visits to Amerindian villages in the area

Waterfalls

Hukou Falls

AKA:	Kettle Spout Falls. As rushing water cascades over the falls, it looks like steam rising from a tea kettle.
LOCATION:	China — on the Huang He (Yellow) River in Shaanxi Province
CLAIM TO FAME:	Only yellow waterfall on Earth
BEST VIEWS:	From the rocky banks of the river below the falls — during the rainy season. Hukou can also be breathtaking in winter when icicles and blocks of ice form.
ACTIVITIES:	Hiking, sightseeing, Chinese cultural activities

Niagara Falls

AKA:	*Onguiaahra*, an Iroquois word from which Niagara is derived. *Les chutes du Niagara* is the French name.
LOCATION:	On the border between New York State and the Canadian province of Ontario — on the Niagara River
CLAIM TO FAME:	It's the most powerful falls in North America. From movies to honeymoon snaps, it's probably the most photographed falls in the world.
BEST VIEWS:	Along walkways bordering the falls on both sides of the river or from the Skylon or Minolta Towers on the Canadian side. Close up and personal — the *Maid of the Mist* boat trip to the whirlpool beneath the falls leaves from the Canadian side.
ACTIVITIES:	Helicopter rides over the falls, a walk behind the falls, or, for a thrill, a 10-minute suspended cable car trip across the Niagara River Gorge below the falls. There are many tourist attractions in the area, from an amusement and marine park to double-decker bus rides, and unique museums.

WORTH A VISIT

JURONG FALLS, SINGAPORE
Tallest artificial falls, located in a rain-forest setting in Jurong Bird Park

GULLFOSS FALLS, ICELAND
A natural waterfall where visitors can walk up and touch the water

Victoria Falls

AKA:	*Mosi- oa-Tunya* — the local Kololo name meaning "The Smoke That Thunders"
LOCATION:	Border between Zambia and Zimbabwe on the Zambezi River
CLAIM TO FAME:	Widest waterfall in the world — one of the Seven Natural Wonders of the World and a UNESCO Heritage Site
BEST VIEWS:	Panoramic views from Knife Edge Bridge or Victoria Bridge; Up close — but more than a little wet — from the pathways along the falls Boiling Pot at the base of the falls — a steep climb down
ACTIVITIES:	The Victoria Falls area is a center for adventure travel — wild white-water rafting on the Zambezi, bungee jumping, river boarding, tandem kayaking, rapelling down the gorge, and more.

IGUAZU FALLS, BORDER OF ARGENTINA AND BRAZIL
A series of 275 falls spread over 2.5 miles in a horseshoe pattern

wrap up

1. Write a caption to accompany each waterfall images.

2. Create a radio or print ad for a holiday at a lodge or hotel near one of the falls described in the fact cards.

WEB CONNECTIONS

Go online to find another spectacular waterfall. Create a fact card for it using the model here.

PERUVIAN ADVENTURE

A VOLUNTEER VACATION

warm up

Have you ever had a unique experience during a school vacation? What would you like to do on the next school break?

What do most students do during their summer holidays? Laze on the beach, work at a summer job, just hang out? Robin Pierro volunteered at an orphanage in Peru. BOLDPRINT interviewed her about her experience.

BOLDPRINT: How did you become interested in a volunteer vacation?

ROBIN PIERRO: I think traveling as a child taught me how to appreciate what I have. My love for traveling and a sudden impulse to "help people" persuaded me to look into volunteer programs abroad.

BP: Why did you choose the orphanage at Cusco?

RP: I chose to go to Cusco because Peru has always fascinated me. It has so much history and such a distinct culture. My grandmother lived in Peru from the age of four until 18 and I've grown up with stories about Peruvian life. Cusco is the archaeological capital of the world and in the areas surrounding the city there are many ancient Inca ruins. I also felt staying in the mountains would be a unique experience.

Robin Pierro

Background–Shutterstock–all other images–courtesy Robin Pierro

BP: What kind of work did you do at the Los Sauces orphanage?

RP: I enjoyed working with the orphans so much and I think I learnt just as much from them as they did from me. I helped the kids with their math homework — I couldn't figure out the Spanish work — and helped out with basic cleaning tasks. Then around 10:00 AM I would take the kids to an abandoned field across the street. Every day, one of the other volunteers would bring some sort of arts and crafts project. The kids loved it! We did everything from painting and drawing to tie-dying and clay sculptures. I also tried to teach them some basic conversational English while they tried to teach me Spanish.

CHECKPOINT

Robin found it easier to learn Spanish from the children. Why do you think this was?

BP: How did the children react to you?

RP: As soon as I walked into the orphanage, I was swamped with children jumping on me, pulling me down, and asking me questions that I didn't understand because my Spanish was a little rusty at that point. The children were used to having volunteers come into the orphanage on a regular basis, so they were very excited to have another person to give them undivided attention. The children were so accepting. The fact that I didn't speak Spanish didn't even matter.

BP: You traveled to Machu Picchu during your fourth week in Peru. How would you describe your trip?

RP: The town of Aguas Calientes is a short bus ride away from Machu Picchu. To get there from Cusco, you must take

Children from Los Sauces

a train ride through the Andes. The train ride was spectacular. Since Machu Picchu is at a lower altitude than Cusco, the air is much warmer and there is far more vegetation. So, not only are the mountains breathtaking, but they are covered in jungle-like vegetation, which only enhances the overall effect.

BP: What was your first impression of Machu Picchu?

RP: When we first arrived, we went through a ticket booth and walked along a short trail. I kept thinking, where is it? Then suddenly, you catch sight of Wayna Picchu, the mountain peak beside Machu Picchu, and a bit of the ruins. You are hit with this amazing postcard view.

Watching the sun slowly sneak over the tips of the mountain and light up the ruins was surreal. The entire experience was very powerful. You just get this incredible feeling when you are standing on the top of a jungle-covered mountain watching the sun rise over a very mysterious ancient city. Mysterious because it is unbelievable how the Inca people actually built Machu Picchu They literally dragged boulders up the side of a mountain and carved them down to fit perfectly

Hiking in the Andes

with one another. It boggles my mind how they were capable of lifting that kind of weight and how every single stone fits precisely with its neighbor. I am still baffled by the idea of Machu Picchu's creation.

CHECKPOINT
How would you describe Machu Picchu from the photographs?

BP: What did you enjoy the most about your experience in Peru?

Machu Picchu

RP: The entire experience was enjoyable so it's hard to pick out one particular aspect. The fact that I was living with a Peruvian family made the entire experience even better. The Cubas were all amazing people. The family was always very accommodating and answered all of my questions. I enjoyed the actual work. The kids were so full of life, love, and laughter. They had a ball, and so did I. It barely felt like work.

BP: What would you say is the most unique aspect of a volunteer vacation?

Llama at Machu Picchu

The Global Crossroads Summer Escapes program is unique in that the volunteers travel throughout Peru for a week, once

surreal: *unbelievable*

Robin at Machu Picchu—courtesy Robin Pierro; all other images—Shutterstock they have finished work at their placements. We flew to the Amazon Jungle region of Peru and spent a few nights in a lodge on the Amazon River. There was only running water for a few hours a day and the lights went out at 9:00 P.M.

The jungle was very beautiful, so lush and green. It rained every day, but only for half an hour and it was a nice refreshing break from the sweltering sun. While in the jungle, we went on a day-long hike (10 hours!) and ran into some wild monkeys. Our jungle guide was literally cutting the path with a machete as we made our way through the thick jungle bush. We also went crocodile hunting and saw some pretty big crocodiles. It was so much fun because everything involved just a little bit of danger and I had great company along the way.

Other than traveling, I found living with the family very unique. They only ate one real meal a day. Breakfast was stale bread and coffee. Lunch was the main meal and everyone came home from work to eat together, and then dinner was once again stale bread and coffee. I found it hard to adjust to one meal a day, so I spent a lot of money in restaurants over the month. I got to try a lot of foods like guinea pig (cuy) that I would never try at home.

It is such a different culture that at first you need time to adjust. But when it comes time to leave you really don't want to.

wrap up

1. List the enjoyable experiences that Robin had in Peru. Write a short article convincing someone to take a volunteer vacation.

2. Write out two additional questions that you would like to ask Robin about her work at the orphanage or about her travels in Peru.

WEB CONNECTIONS

Go online to find information about another volunteer vacation opportunity. Create a fact sheet about the program.

Robin at Machu Picchu

PHOTO SAFARI

Safari elephants—Getty Images/Stone/Mitch Kezar/697763-001; all other images—Shutterstock, istockphoto.

NAIROBI, KENYA

There were five of us — three Americans and two Canadians — ready for the adventure of a lifetime — an African safari. Our guide, Nelson, would drive us in a minibus. We were loaded with luggage and cameras of all types — digital, video, 35-millimeter …

warm up

Imagine that you have a chance to go on a photo safari in East Africa. What animals would you expect to see?

DAY 1

OSTRICH CROSSING

We weren't far on our way when we came to a stop for this ostrich. This huge bird is quite a sight when it runs — head up, behind out — and those skinny legs! It runs on its toes and it can really run — up to 40 mph. Nelson told us that only the cheetah can run faster. Our ostrich was almost sauntering, obviously not afraid of us.

MASAI MARA GAME RESERVE IN KENYA

Masai Mara was the first reserve that we visited. It's part of the huge Rift Valley and is home to the big five — elephants, buffalo, rhinos, lions, and leopards. But Masai Mara is also noted for the large herds of animals, such as these zebras, that gather at waterholes.

 DAY 2

BALLOON RIDES OVER THE MARA

Some of us signed up for this balloon ride across the Mara. At times, we were as high as 1,500 feet above the plain. At other times, we descended to get close-up views of wildlife. It was awesome! Nelson met us when we landed and we continued looking for game in an open jeep.

MASAI DANCERS

Later we were entertained by Masai dancers in their traditional red robes and elaborate bead work. The music was all-voice and the dance was graceful at times, aggressive at other times — with jumping and hopping about.

DAY 3

SERENGETI NATIONAL PARK, RIFT VALLEY, TANZANIA

This is one of the world's largest animal sanctuaries and a UNESCO World Heritage Site. We were able to get close-ups of giraffes, Thomson Gazelles, and this smiling hippo.

DAY 4

NGORONGORO CRATER

Nelson told us that the Ngorongoro Crater was formed when a volcano exploded about two million years ago. We stayed at a lodge on the rim of the crater, 2,000 feet above its floor. I met this zebra while walking from our cottage to the main lodge for dinner.

DAY 5

OPEN JEEP RIDE INTO THE CRATER

Animals are less people-shy here than at the other reserves we visited so I was able to get more close-ups. Nelson seems to know exactly where to find the animals like these elephants and cheetahs.

DAY 6

LAKE MANYARA, TANZANIA

What a spectacular sight — hundreds of pink flamingos taking flight as we approached the lake. The lake is one of many soda lakes in the Rift Valley that support thousands of birds. Soda lakes have large amounts of sodium carbonate. High bacteria levels in the lakes give flamingos their beautiful pink color.

These tree lions are also unique to this area. They seem to enjoy lazy afternoons just hanging out.

DAY 7

BACK TO NAIROBI

Lorna managed to get this great photo of a baboon and her baby as we drove back to Nairobi and the end of our safari. Nelson was a wonderful driver and guide and we have great memories and hundreds of photographs of our safari.

wrap up

1. Imagine that you were on this photo safari and write a journal entry for one of the days in the itinerary.

2. Study the photographs and write a sentence describing each one.

WEB CONNECTIONS

Use the Web to find information about the Masai. Create a fact card for this cultural group.

Calling All CHOCOHOLICS

How much do you like chocolate? Poll your group or class to find out what the most popular chocolate treats are.

*O*ut There — *Travel* offers a world tour for those of us who love to indulge in chocolate.

The first stop is Oaxaca, the chocolate capital of Mexico — the place where it all began. The ancient Maya and the Aztecs were using cocoa beans as currency and to make chocolate drinks as far back as 600 C.E. Today, their descendants in Mexico still cherish chocolate and use it in baking and in a sauce called *mole*. Mole is a mixture of chocolate and spices used to flavor meat and chicken. Hot chocolate is preferred over coffee and this drink is made from a paste called *molienda*, a combination of cocoa beans, sugar, and cinnamon.

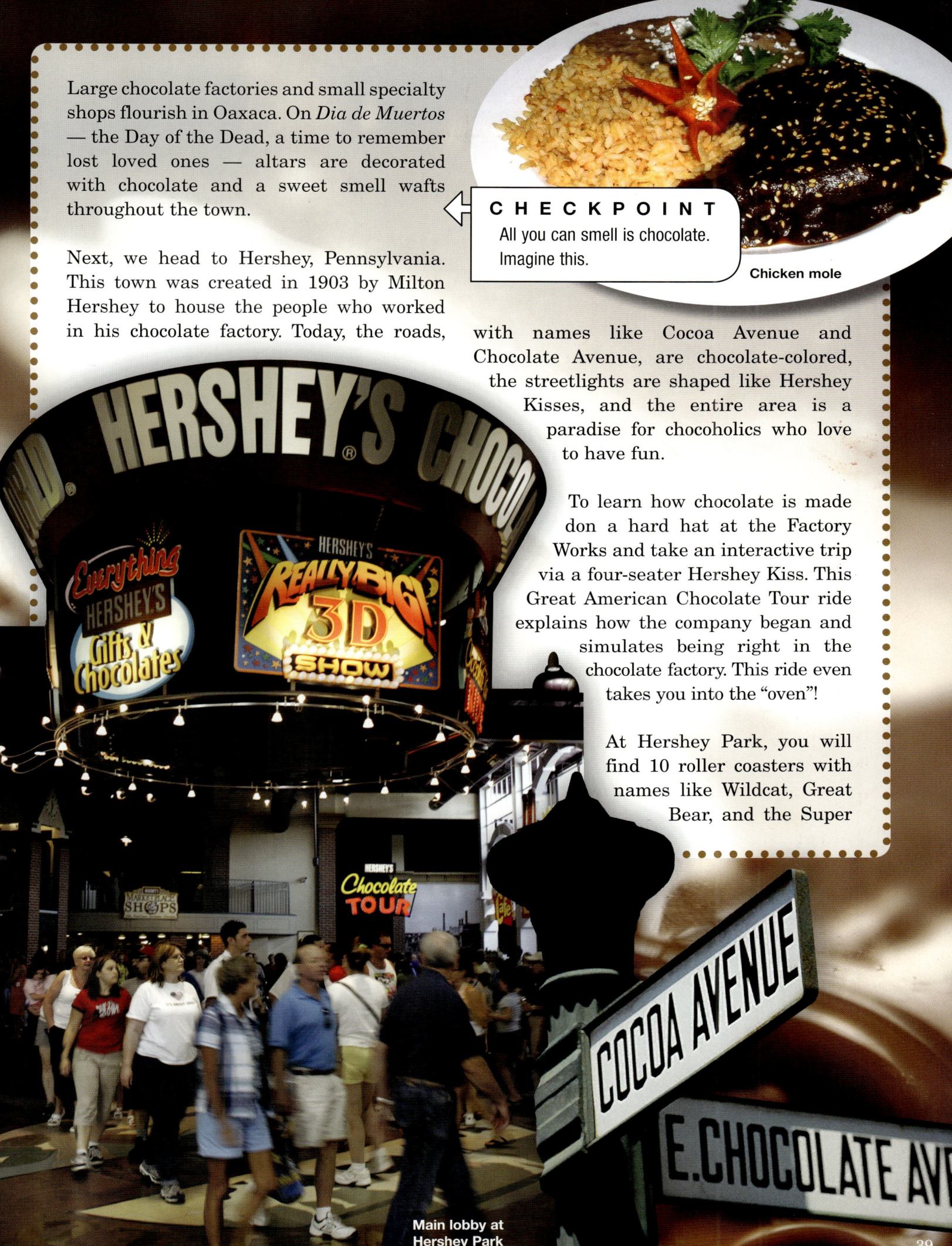

Large chocolate factories and small specialty shops flourish in Oaxaca. On *Dia de Muertos* — the Day of the Dead, a time to remember lost loved ones — altars are decorated with chocolate and a sweet smell wafts throughout the town.

Next, we head to Hershey, Pennsylvania. This town was created in 1903 by Milton Hershey to house the people who worked in his chocolate factory. Today, the roads, with names like Cocoa Avenue and Chocolate Avenue, are chocolate-colored, the streetlights are shaped like Hershey Kisses, and the entire area is a paradise for chocoholics who love to have fun.

To learn how chocolate is made don a hard hat at the Factory Works and take an interactive trip via a four-seater Hershey Kiss. This Great American Chocolate Tour ride explains how the company began and simulates being right in the chocolate factory. This ride even takes you into the "oven"!

At Hershey Park, you will find 10 roller coasters with names like Wildcat, Great Bear, and the Super

CHECKPOINT
All you can smell is chocolate. Imagine this.

Chicken mole

Main lobby at Hershey Park

Dooper Looper. After a day at the park, head back to the Factory Works and order a chocolate dessert made just the way you want it.

Still hungry for more chocolate adventures? Then Cadbury World in England is the place to visit. The Cadbury Chocolate Company was started by John Cadbury in 1824. Like Milton Hershey, John's sons, George and Richard Cadbury, built a countryside town to house their chocolate factory workers. Called Bournville, this village today offers a fun way for the whole family to learn all about chocolate. The Aztec Forest, featuring tropical plants and waterfalls, tells the history of chocolate using 3-D shows. You can also see chocolate being made and enjoy samples. There are two new attractions — Essence and Purple Planet — where you can make your own concoctions, grow cocoa beans, or go to the Cadbury space station for virtual-reality fun. More than 500,000 people visit Cadbury World every year. This theme park provides education, fun, and best of all, loads of chocolate.

CHECKPOINT
What do you think "concoctions" means?

England also offers Alton Towers, a theme park near Manchester. This attraction features the Oblivion roller coaster with its vertical drop as well as the Charlie and The Chocolate Factory ride. A visit to this destination takes you into the magical world of Charlie Bucket, the winner of a Golden Ticket, who embarks on a wondrous journey to meet Willie Wonka. This ride is based on a book written by famous children's author, Roald Dahl.

CHECKPOINT
Have you read the books or seen the movies?

Sitting in a boat, you travel down a chocolate river into the heart of the factory. This is the world's first multisensory ride that takes you on a 3-D tour. The journey ends in the Great Glass Elevator, which tilts every which way before finally exploding through the roof of the factory!

Chocolate lovers should also travel to Europe to savor their favorite food. Brussels, the capital of Belgium, is called the chocolate capital of the world. This city has more than 2,000 chocolate shops as well as museums dealing solely with this treat. Paris, France, has a week-long chocolate festival as does Periugia, Italy, which also boasts the world's only Choccohotel. In this building, everything from the rooms to the meals is based on chocolate.

Land-based travel doesn't interest you? Try a chocolate-themed cruise with decadent desserts. There are literally dozens of chocolate adventures to choose from. And the best thing of all? Chocolate, especially the dark variety, is actually good for you. Feel like a chocolate bar?

Oblivion roller coaster at Alton Towers

CHECKPOINT
Do you know why dark chocolate is good for you?

All images–Shutterstock, istockphoto

wrap up

1. Use an online or book atlas to locate all the places mentioned in the article.

2. From the article and the images, decide which chocolate destination you would most like to visit. Research the place further and write out an itinerary for a one-day visit.

WEB CONNECTIONS

Use the Web to find other foods enjoyed by the Aztecs, the Inca, and the Maya. Record these in a chart and note the foods that you have tried.

SWIMMING IS

warm up

Why do you think swimming would be "strange in the Dead Sea"?

STRANGE IN THE DEAD SEA

BY JULIA DIMON

Standing on the shore of the Dead Sea, I dipped my hand into a bucket, pulled out a clump of dark sludgy mud and smeared it all over my face. Apparently this is the thing to do when visiting the Dead Sea, a body of water shared by both Jordan and Israel.

FYI

The Dead Sea is the lowest spot on Earth – 1,370 feet below sea level.

Since Dead Sea mud has natural medicinal properties, it leaves the skin feeling smooth and healthy. This free beauty treatment was just what I needed after trekking through Jordan's many dusty archaeological sites.

Slathered head to toe in mud, with only the whites of my eyes and a bit of pink bikini showing, I looked like a swamp monster. After 15 minutes, I showered and looked human again.

Post mud, I joined a dozen other sunbathers in the healing waters of the famous Dead Sea. Due to its obscene levels of salt, this natural spa is devoid of marine life.

"Swimming" in the Dead Sea

CHECKPOINT
Imagine swimming here.

feels strange. Lying on your stomach, your feet pop out of the water, you feel off-balance and are forced to doggy-paddle. Lying on your back, it's as if you're on an inflatable mattress. In either position, you can't really swim, you just float.

Thanks to those high salt levels, every little cut, blister or scrape stings like a swarm of wasps. I experienced this first hand when I splashed water into my own eye. Man, did it burn.

A friend dared me to taste the water; I stuck out my tongue and lapped it up. The taste was so indescribably vile, I wished for water-in-the-eye instead. With two handicapped senses, I dragged my silky smooth skin out of the water, ordered a cold [drink] and watched the sun set ….

wrap up

As Julia, send an e-mail to a friend describing your swimming experience in the Dead Sea.

WEB CONNECTIONS

Go online to find more information about tourism in the Dead Sea area. In a small group, create a three-fold travel brochure about the area.

Touring Thailand

By Maeve Gallagher

warm up

Before you start to read, use an atlas or the Web to locate Thailand.

FYI

Thai means "freedom" in the Thai language.

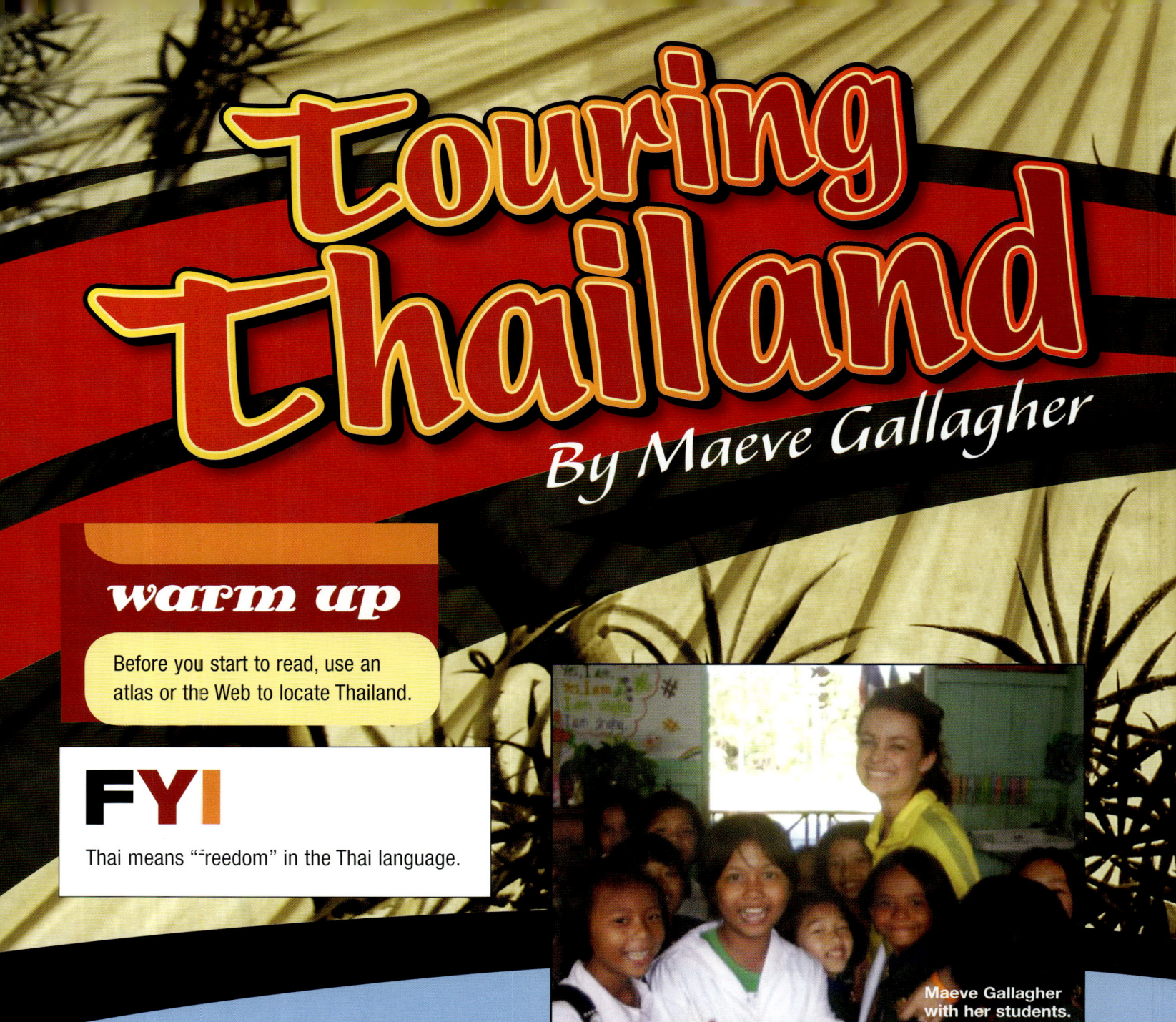

Maeve Gallagher with her students.

I was lucky enough to spend my four-month long summer teaching English and traveling through Thailand. Before I left, I dreamed about white sands and crystal clear water. What I didn't know was how much more there was to Thailand — the culture, the politics, the geography ….

When I arrived in Bangkok, the capital of Thailand, I was overwhelmed. I didn't speak Thai and I had never experienced heat like the heat that hit me when I left the comfort of the air-conditioned airport. I spent my first week experiencing all that Bangkok had to offer. I visited a lot of Buddhist temples, but the two most spectacular were Wat Pho and Wat Arun. "Wat" is the Thai word for temple. The first temple, Wat Pho, is the biggest temple in Bangkok. It has the largest reclining Buddha in the world, about 150 feet long and 50 feet high! As if that wasn't impressive enough, the temple has the most beautiful stone guard statues and large stupas, which apparently hold relics of the Buddha himself. Wat Arun is the other famous temple in Bangkok. Wat Arun actually means 'The Temple of Dawn." I loved how colorful it was.

stupas: *dome-shaped structure or mound*

Wat Arun "The Temple of Dawn"

Largest reclining buddha

Wat Pho

Bangkok is also famous for its shopping. Because the baht, compared to the American dollar, is relatively cheap, shopping in the huge shopping malls in Bangkok was definitely something I never tired of! The Paragon Shopping Center in Siam Square, Bangkok's shopping district is the most extravagant shopping mall I had ever seen — it even has a full aquarium.

I dedicated a full day to the National Museum in Bangkok. Thailand has such a rich history that spending the day at the museum — seeing relics from invasions that occurred a thousand years ago and the armor that Thai soldiers wore — was a real learning experience.

CHECKPOINT
What do you think someone could learn from these items?

baht: *Thai currency worth about $.03*
extravagant: *luxurious*

Because I worked only four days per week, I was very fortunate to be able to travel a lot on my time off. One of the best weekends of my trip was when I traveled to Chiang Mai, the second largest city in Thailand. It is located in the north of the country. I was only there a short time, but I was able to see a lot of sights. I rented a motorcycle and traveled around for a day through Doi Inthanon, the highest mountain in Thailand. I visited Wat Doi Suthep, which is a beautiful temple that is hidden on top of Doi Inthanon. I had to climb more than 300 stairs just to get there. But the view was worth every step.

CHECKPOINT
About how many stories would this be?

On the way down from the temple, I stopped to see the Vachiratharn waterfalls, which are part of a national park and are breathtaking. Chiang Mai has a famous night bazaar that would take several days to completely cover.

Siam Square

Vachiratharn Falls

All images–Shutterstock, istockphoto

Eating noodle soup and fried bananas at the bazaar and buying local crafts was a night well spent.

In the province where I taught English and lived for a few days of the week, there was a famous floating market called the Amphawa Floating Market. Going every Sunday became a fun tradition, and buying a week's worth of fruits from the vendors in the boats along the Maeklong River never lost its charm.

The last two weeks of my time in Thailand was devoted completely to travel and I was able to spend the time on the islands in southern Thailand. I spent a few days in the city of Ayutthaya, which is the former ancient capital of Thailand founded around 1350 C.E. and home to some of the oldest and most beautiful temples and buildings in the country. The city was burned in 1767 during warfare with the Burmese, and Bangkok was later made the capital.

Full Moon holiday is celebrated in a less traditional way, with thousands of people from all over the world coming to the beach and dancing for the whole night. The Full Moon Party occurs every full moon, and the particular one I went to was attended by about 14,000 people — all on one beach! I met a lot of interesting characters that night.

After spending four months in Thailand eating the wonderful food (Pad Thai and spicy papaya salad were my favorites.), meeting the people, and seeing the most beautiful sights in the world, it is still difficult to explain how much Thailand meant to me. Coming home to Canada was bittersweet, as I was excited about seeing my family and friends, but leaving a place that had shaped me so much in so little time was difficult.

CHECKPOINT
What do you think "bittersweet" means?

I can't wait to go back to Thailand one day, and in the meantime, I wouldn't trade the memories of my time there for anything.

Amphawa Floating Market

wrap up

1. Imagine that you were traveling with Maeve. Write three or four journal entries describing your experiences.

2. Check out the photographs. Choose two and write a short description for each one.

WEB CONNECTIONS

Use the Web to find information about Buddha. Write a short biography for him.

ACKNOWLEDGMENTS

The publisher gratefully acknowledges the following for permission to reprint copyrighted material in this book.

Every reasonable effort has been made to trace the owners of copyrighted material and to make due acknowledgment. Any errors or omissions drawn to our attention will be gladly rectified in future editions.

Julia Dimon: "Swimming is Strange in the Dead Sea," from *Metro*, published Oct. 5, 2005. Permission courtesy of Julia Dimon.

Maeve Gallagher: "Touring Thailand." Permission courtesy of Maeve Gallagher.

Robin Pierro: "Peruvian Adventure — A Volunteer Vacation." Permission courtesy of Robin Pierro.

Catherine Pike: "Mule Ride with a View," from *Toronto Star*, published on March 4, 2006. Permission courtesy of Catherine Pike.